Tender Moments

TENDER MOMENTS

Selected by
Ben Whitley

HALLMARK EDITIONS

Tender Moments

No bird soars too high,
if he soars with his own wings.

WILLIAM BLAKE

When I heard the church
bells ring
I thought I heard the voice
of God.

ALBERT SCHWEITZER

If I had but two loaves of bread,
I would sell one and buy
hyacinth, for they would feed
my soul.

The KORAN

To see a world in a grain of sand
And a heaven in a wild flower:
Hold infinity in the palm of
    your hand,
And eternity in an hour.

No man is an island, entire of itself; every man is a piece of the continent, a part of the main; if a clod be washed away by the sea, Europe is the less, as well as if a promontory were, as well as if a manor of thy friends or of thine own were; any man's death diminishes me, because I am involved in mankind; and therefore never send to know for whom the bell tolls; it tolls for thee.

JOHN DONNE

I keep my ideals, because in
spite of everything I still believe
that people are really good
at heart.

ANNE FRANK

Happiness is as a butterfly, which,
when pursued, is always just
beyond your grasp, but which,
if you will sit down quietly,
may alight upon you.

What is beautiful is a joy for
all seasons and a possession
for all eternity.

OSCAR WILDE

What is beautiful is good,
and who is good
will soon also be beautiful.

SAPPHO

A friend is the present you
give yourself.

ROBERT LOUIS STEVENSON

If thou findest a good man,
rise up early in the morning
to go to him, and let thy feet
wear the steps of his door.

THE APOCRYPHAL BOOK
OF ECCLESIASTICUS

As rivers have their source in
some far off fountain, so the
human spirit has its source.
To find this fountain of spirit is
to learn the secret of heaven
and earth.

LAO-TSE

The most I can do for my friend
is simply to be his friend.

HENRY DAVID THOREAU

Time is not measured
by the passing of the years,
but by what one does, what one feels,
and what one achieves.

JAWAHARLAL NEHRU

I want it said of me by those
who knew me best, that I always
plucked a thistle and planted
a flower where I thought a
flower would grow.

ABRAHAM LINCOLN

Those who bring sunshine to the
lives of others cannot keep
it from themselves.

SIR JAMES BARRIE

If a man does not keep pace
with his companions, perhaps it
is because he hears a different
drummer. Let him step to the
music he hears, however
measured or far away.

HENRY DAVID THOREAU

I shall not pass this way again.
Any good thing that I can do, or
any kindness that I can show,
let me do it now! Let me not
defer it or neglect it. For I shall
not pass this way again.

STEPHEN GRELLET

The world was beautiful....
The moon and the stars were
beautiful, the brook, the shore,
the forest and rock...the flower
and butterfly were beautiful.

HERMANN HESSE

Nothing in life is to be feared.
It is only to be understood.

MARIE CURIE

Walk on a rainbow trail; walk on
a trail of song,
and all about you
will be beauty.

NAVAJO SONG

Write on your hearts that every
day is the best day of the year.

RALPH WALDO EMERSON

What a thing friendship is —
World without end!

ROBERT BROWNING

Beauty is silent eloquence.

FRENCH PROVERB

Some men see things as they are and say, why. I dream things that never were and say, why not.

ROBERT F. KENNEDY

If I keep a green bough
in my heart,
the singing bird will come.

CHINESE PROVERB

We cannot tell the precise moment when friendship is formed. As in filling a vessel drop by drop, there is at last a drop which makes it run over; so in a series of kindnesses there is at last one which makes the heart run over.

JAMES BOSWELL

It is only important to love the world…to regard the world and ourselves and all beings with love, admiration and respect.

HERMANN HESSE

I discovered the secret of
the sea in meditation upon
a dewdrop.

KAHLIL GIBRAN

Friends create the world anew
each day. Without their loving
care, courage would not suffice
to keep hearts strong for life.

HELEN KELLER

To me every hour of the light
and dark is a miracle.
Every cubic inch of space is
a miracle.

WALT WHITMAN